Machines at work
AIRPLANE

LONDON, NEW YORK, MUNICH,
MELBOURNE, and DELHI

Written and edited by Caroline Bingham
Designed by Cheryl Telfer
Managing editor Susan Leonard
Managing art editor Clare Shedden
US editor Christine Heilman
Jacket designer Emy Manby
Jacket editor Mariza O'Keeffe
Picture researcher Carolyn Clerkin
Production Lucy Baker
DTP Designer Almudena Díaz
Consultant Michael Allaby

2659254

First American Edition, 2003
06 07 10 9 8 7 6 5 4 3 2

Published in the United States by DK Publishing, Inc.
375 Hudson Street, New York, New York 100014

Library of Congress Cataloging-in-Publication Data

Bingham, Caroline, 1962-
Airplane / Caroline Bingham.-- 1st American ed.
p. cm. -- (Machines at work)
Includes index.
Summary: Introduces assorted airplanes and other flying machines,
including gliders, helicopters, and space shuttles.
ISBN 0-7894-9222-9 (PLC) 0-7566-1788-X (PB)
1. Airplanes--Juvenile literature. [1. Airplanes. 2. Flying
machines.] I. Title. II. Series: Machines at work (DK Publishing, Inc.)

TL547 .B444 2003
629.133'3--dc21
2002014866

Color reproduction by GRB Editrice, S.r.l., Verona, Italy
Printed and bound in China by Toppan Printing Co., Ltd.

see our complete product line at
www.dk.com

Contents

Getting ready

An **airport** is a busy place, with airplanes constantly arriving and departing. Each plane has to be checked, refueled, and cleaned— often in less than an hour.

Get ready to board
At a large airport, the planes line up at gates. This is where passengers get on and off.

An international airport may see more than 200,000 passengers pass through each day.

In with the cargo
Scissor-lift machines are used to load and unload a large plane with all kinds of containers. Some will contain food for the flight.

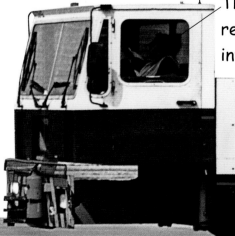

The tug driver reverses the tug into position.

More than 20 vehicles may come and go to service a large airplane.

BRITISH AIRWAYS

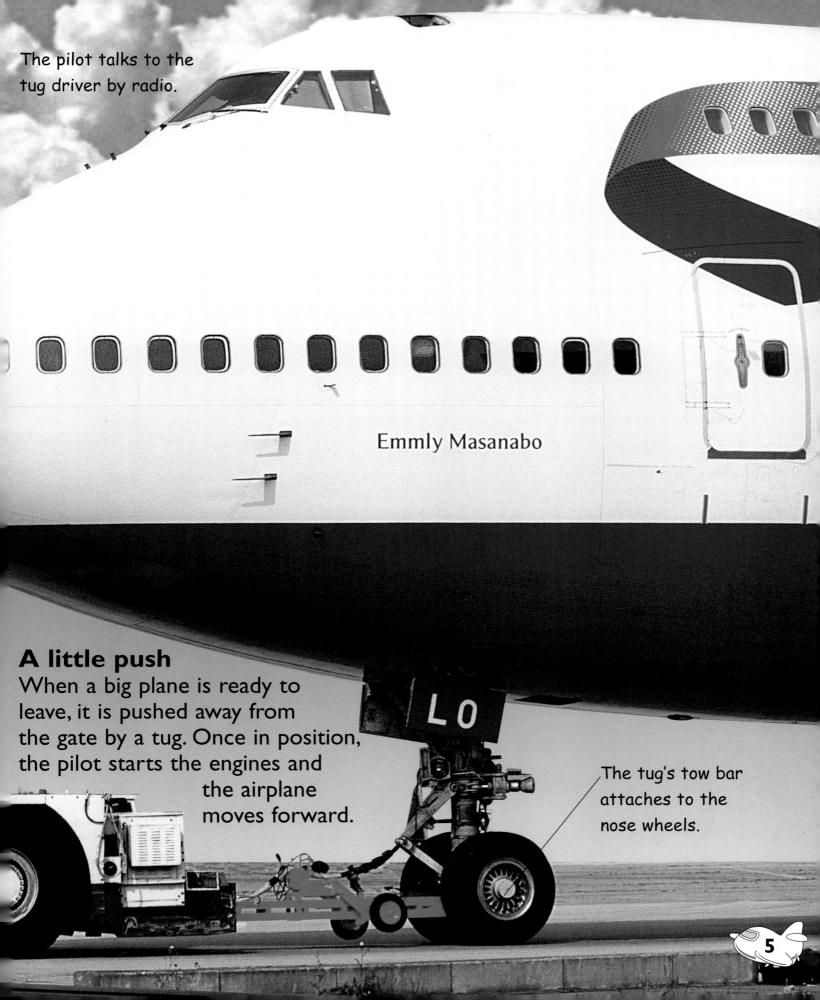

The pilot talks to the tug driver by radio.

Emmly Masanabo

A little push

When a big plane is ready to leave, it is pushed away from the gate by a tug. Once in position, the pilot starts the engines and the airplane moves forward.

The tug's tow bar attaches to the nose wheels.

Taking off

As an airplane roars down the runway, air rushes over and under the **wings** in such a way that the plane is forced up.

Traffic jam

At a busy airport, airplanes may be flying in and out every minute. They sometimes have to line up and wait for permission to move, or taxi, onto the runway.

Wheels are drawn back into compartments in the fuselage.

Flaps are tilted down to increase the wing's curve.

A runway is often more than 2 miles (3 kilometers) in length.

Fasten your seat belts! Get ready for takeoff.

Staying in touch

When waiting to land, an airplane is in constant contact with the control tower. The plane will appear on the control tower's computer screens as a tiny dot.

Get ready to land.

In control

It's easy to spot an airport's control tower—it's a tall building and often a funny shape. The people inside decide when each plane can take off or land.

Up with the wheels

The wheels (or landing gear) are pulled up quickly after takeoff. This lowers drag—the resistance pulling against the aircraft.

Flying high

Imagine sitting at the controls of
a large airliner. The panel in front
of you is packed with buttons, switches,
screens, lights, and dials. A **pilot** has
to understand what each one does.

These dials provide
information about
the engine.

Which one first?

The basic flight controls—the
yoke, wing flap control, and
throttles—are within easy
reach of the pilot and copilot.

Control yoke

The 767 flight deck was the first two- (instead of three-) person flight deck on a twin-aisle airplane.

Thanks to computers, modern 747s have just 365 controls. The first models had 971 flight deck controls.

Landing and taxi light switches

Screens have replaced the banks of dials in older airplanes.

Make way for the jumbo!

A **Boeing 747** is the largest passenger airplane in the world. It can carry about **400** passengers. That's why it's known as a jumbo. It's a giant among airplanes.

A long stretch

The top of a 747's tailfin is 63 feet (19 meters) above the ground. Maintenance workers use machines called cherry pickers to get there.

Fuel is carried in the wings, in the central section between the wings, and in the tail.

Packing it in

A fully loaded 747 will have 416 passengers on board, along with around 600 pieces of luggage in the hold, and more than 800 meals.

747s are so big that they have a second floor— and stairs to get to it.

Where do you sit?
There are three seating areas in a typical 747— and the more you pay, the more space you get.

Ten passengers can sit side-by-side in the economy section.

At 7 inches (19 centimeters) thick, the fuselage skin is almost as wide as a page from this book.

It's a fact
🛩 The 120-foot (36-meter) distance of the Wright brothers' first flight could have taken place within the 150-foot (45-meter) economy section of a 747.

Where's the engine?

Imagine soaring through the air without the sound of an engine. That's what it's like when you fly in a **glider**.

How does it stay up?

Once in the air, a glider pilot looks for thermals—warm pockets of rising air—to climb. A glider can stay up for hours by riding these thermals.

Towing a glider is called an aero-tow.

A helping hand

A glider has to be helped into the air. One way of doing this is to drag it up behind a powered plane. A long cable connects the two aircraft and is released in the air.

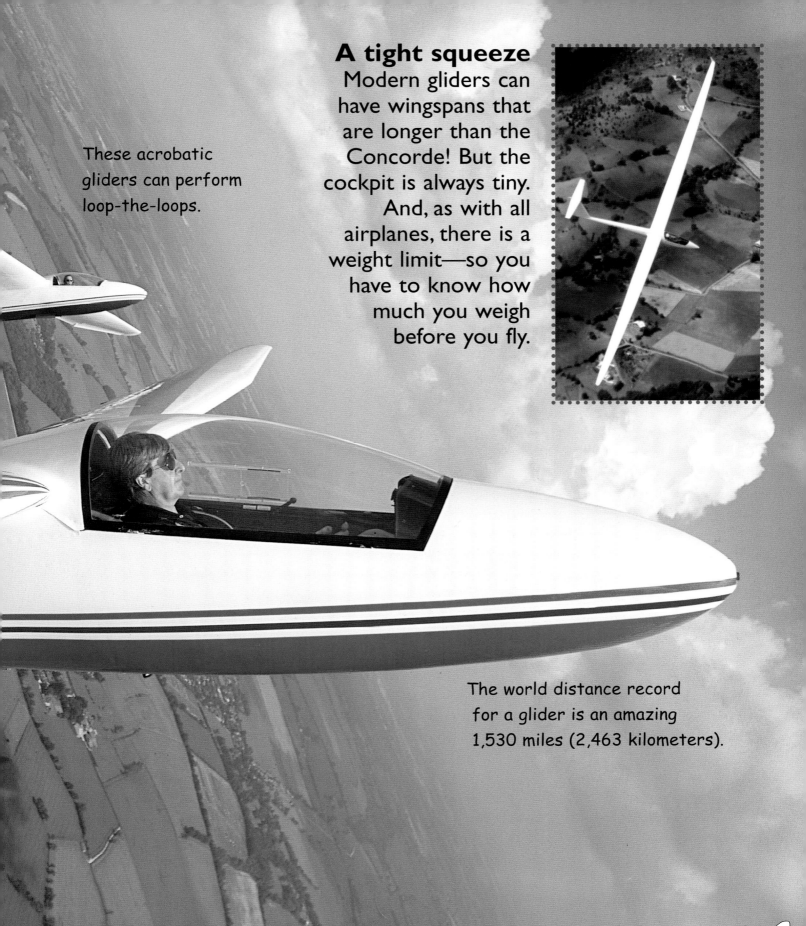

These acrobatic gliders can perform loop-the-loops.

A tight squeeze
Modern gliders can have wingspans that are longer than the Concorde! But the cockpit is always tiny. And, as with all airplanes, there is a weight limit—so you have to know how much you weigh before you fly.

The world distance record for a glider is an amazing 1,530 miles (2,463 kilometers).

Thirsty beasts

Some military planes are equipped to **refuel** in midair. Picking up the hose to "fill 'er up" takes a lot of skill.

The rim of the drogue basket inflates in the air.

Aviation fuel is pumped along the fuel line at about 1,200 gallons (4,500 liters) a minute.

A speedy exchange
The two airplanes fly only yards apart, but are moving three times as fast as a car on a highway.

A steady workhorse
Aircraft chosen as tankers have to be strong and dependable. The VC-10, shown here refueling a Tornado, is a good example. It is a converted passenger plane.

Refueling can take place from a wing-mounted refueling pod.

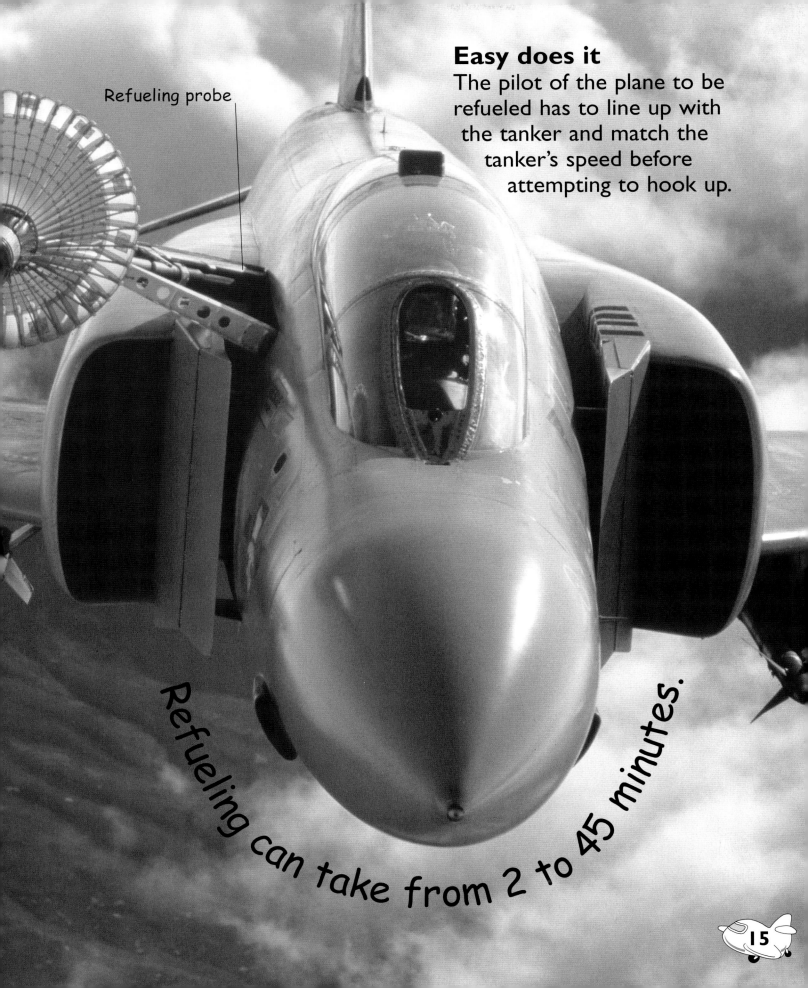

Refueling probe

Easy does it
The pilot of the plane to be refueled has to line up with the tanker and match the tanker's speed before attempting to hook up.

Refueling can take from 2 to 45 minutes.

How does a helicopter fly?

About **500** years ago an Italian artist and scientist named Leonardo da Vinci sketched an idea for a **helicopter**. Yet the first helicopter did not fly until the **1930s**.

It has two!
The Chinook transport helicopter is powered by two engines. These turn the 60-foot- (18-meter-) diameter three-blade rotors.

Keep on spinning
Instead of wings, a helicopter has long rotor blades that spin around to pull the aircraft up into the air. They are driven by an engine above the cabin.

Helicopter rotors spin around about 500 times a minute.

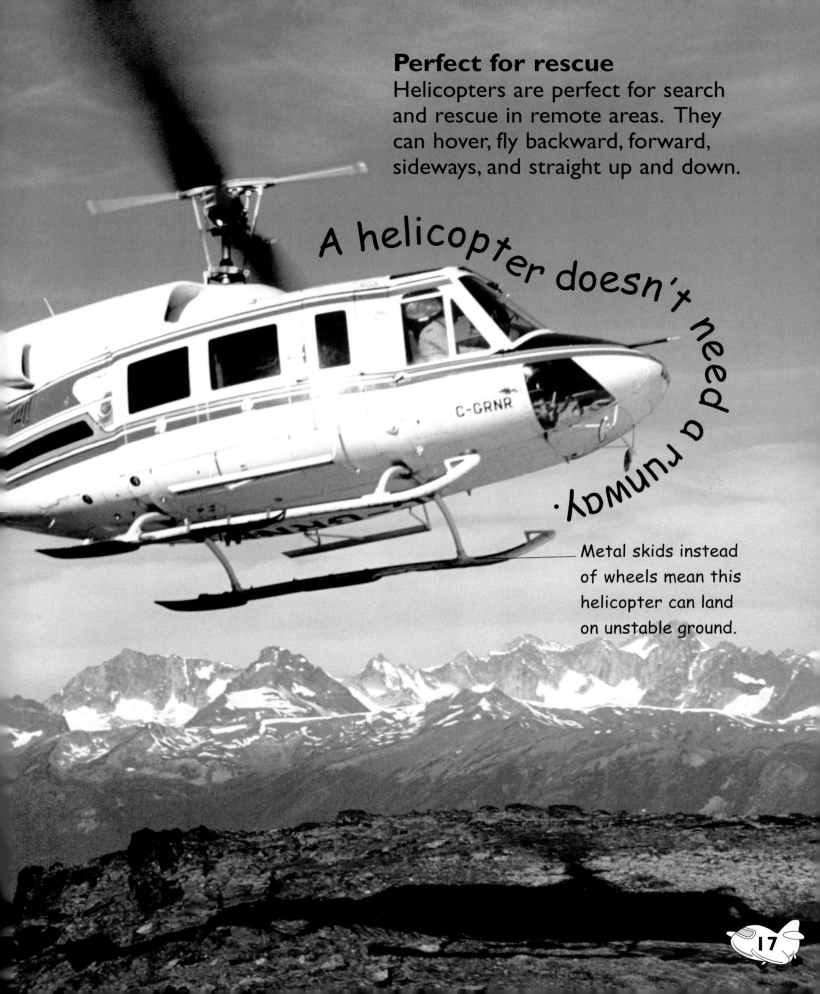

Perfect for rescue

Helicopters are perfect for search and rescue in remote areas. They can hover, fly backward, forward, sideways, and straight up and down.

A helicopter doesn't need a runway.

Metal skids instead of wheels mean this helicopter can land on unstable ground.

C-GRNR

17

Air acrobats

Stunt planes are the acrobats of the air. Whether flying in groups or alone, they give an incredible display.

Airplanes with two wings are known as biplanes.

Leaving a trail

Aerobatic planes often release vapor trails, which stream out behind them. Sometimes these are dyed red or blue.

18

Wing to wing

Stunt planes flying together can make many different formations in the sky, with wingtips nearly touching.

From spin to roll to loop-the-loop.

The pilot of each plane is in constant radio contact with the other pilots in the display team.

Just taking a stroll...

Helped by a safety harness, wing walkers perform death-defying stunts on the wings of a plane.

Little flyers

An ultralight is a tiny one- or two-person aircraft with a small engine and a propeller. The **pilot** sits in a trike.

Just hanging around

Ultralights developed from the sport of hang gliding, where a person flies under a huge wing. Body movement controls the hang glider's direction.

A high flyer

Once up, an ultralight can stay in the air for several hours, and reach about 15,000 feet (900 meters).

One ultralight has managed to stay up for

A comfortable chair
The pilot sits in a small seat, on top of three fixed wheels. The wheels are needed for takeoff and landing. An ultralight pilot wears a helmet.

The metal frame is made of lightweight aluminum.

565 miles (1,071 km).

It's a fact
Takeoff happens at 20 mph (32 km/h).

Top speed is about 60 mph (100 km/h).

An ultralight can fly for about four hours.

Record breaker

This amazing aircraft first flew in the 1960s. It is known as the **Blackbird** because of its black coating and unusual shape. It is the **fastest jet** aircraft ever.

A Blackbird pilot wears a suit that is a little like an astronaut's. It seals the pilot inside.

The parachute is known as a drag chute because it drags the air to slow the plane.

It's cold outside
This suit protects the pilot in case he has to eject. At the height the plane flies, the air is too thin to breathe and too cold to survive without help.

Stop, stop, S-T-O-P
Blackbird touches down at such a high speed that it needs help from a parachute to stop! The parachute stops the plane within about 1,100 yards (1,000 meters).

Tiny iron balls in the paint mean the plane cannot be seen on radar.

Stop that leak!

On the way up, fuel streaks out of the Blackbird's tanks. Once the plane heats up, the metal expands enough to seal the tanks.

23

A watery landing

Not all airplanes are built to land on a hard runway. **Amphibians** and **seaplanes** land on water.

Ready for snow
In areas of heavy snow, airplanes can even be equipped with skis!

Echoes of a gull
This large amphibious plane is a Beriev Be-12. The gull-shaped wings are mounted at the top of the fuselage, keeping the engines clear of water spray.

The four-blade propeller is 16 foot (4.85 meters) in diameter.

The plane could reach the top of the Eiffel Tower in France in just 20 seconds.

Float on by
In areas with wide expanses of water, small four-seater passenger planes have floats instead of wheels.

Blast off!

A space shuttle roars up, leaving a massive **vapor trail** behind. It can make repeated trips to and from space, delivering and repairing **satellites.**

Made up of parts

The space shuttle is made up of four main parts. The orbiter rides on the back of a gigantic fuel tank and two booster rockets.

USA
United States

Take off!

The space shuttle blasts off and moves upward, away from the launch pad. Hot gases escape from the rocket, forcing the shuttle upward.

The huge fuel tank falls away about eight minutes into the flight.

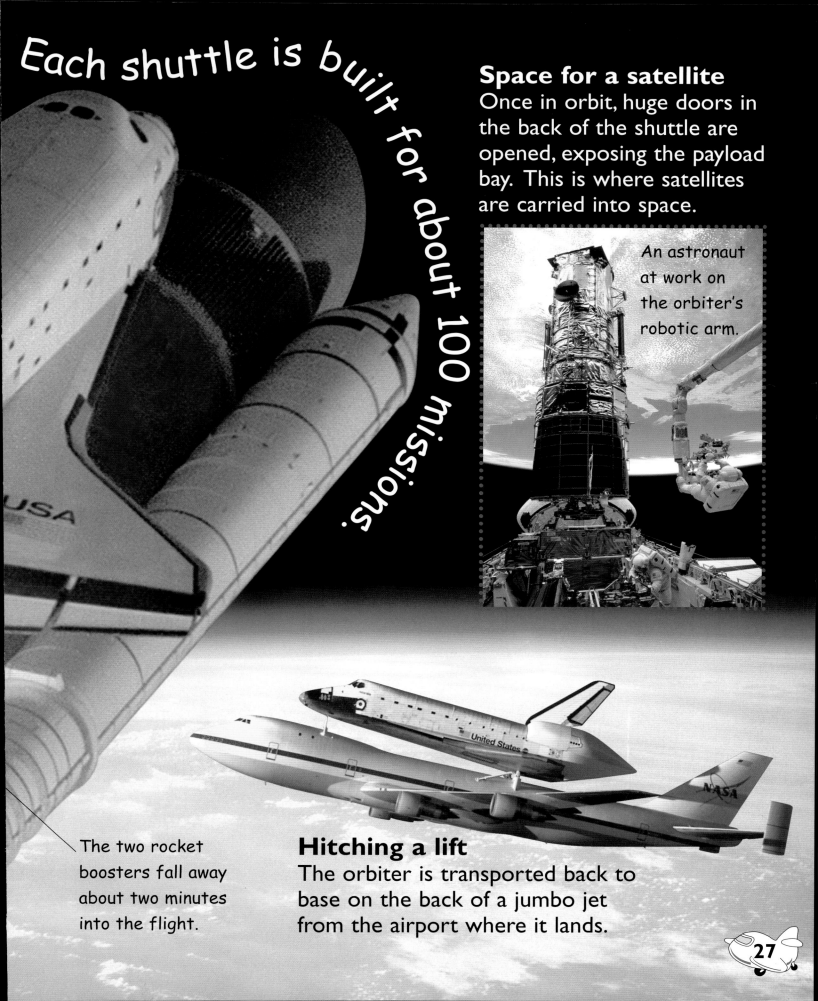

Each shuttle is built for about 100 missions.

Space for a satellite
Once in orbit, huge doors in the back of the shuttle are opened, exposing the payload bay. This is where satellites are carried into space.

An astronaut at work on the orbiter's robotic arm.

The two rocket boosters fall away about two minutes into the flight.

Hitching a lift
The orbiter is transported back to base on the back of a jumbo jet from the airport where it lands.

A model of one of Leonardo's sketches.

Days of old

The fight to claim the skies has come a long way since the first **powered** flight by the Wright brothers' *Flyer*, which took place on December 17, 1903.

First attempts

Leonardo da Vinci (1452–1519) spent many hours sketching bird and bat flight. He also sketched ideas for fabric-winged flying machines.

The S.E.5a could reach 138 mph (222 km/h).

Wright Flyer

Wilbur and Orville Wright were fascinated by flight from a young age. Their *Flyer* flew just four times before it crashed and was destroyed, but it was an incredible achievement. Five people witnessed the 12-second flight.

The RAF S.E.5a was the finest British World War I fighter aircraft.

Getting bigger

The Lockheed Constellation shows how quickly aircraft developed. By the 1950s, Constellations were carrying **99 passengers** across ocean routes at cruising speeds of **327 mph (526 km/h)**.

Each engine had more than 200 times the power of the **Flyer**.

A biplane has two wings and an open cockpit.

It's a fact

The **Flyer** had a 12-hp engine. A modern family car has an engine that is 10 times as powerful.

Biplanes took to the skies in huge numbers in World War I (1914–1918).

One wing or two?

Biplanes are an important stage in the history of flight. Early planes had thin wood and fabric wings. Struts and bracing wire between two wings increased their strength.

Picture gallery

Blackbird

To heat their food, Blackbird pilots held the packets against the hot cockpit windows.

Seaplane

A seaplane's runway is the water. A small seaplane needs about 1 mile (1.6 km) of clear water on which to land.

Glider

The world altitude record for a glider is just under 50,000 feet (15,000 meters).

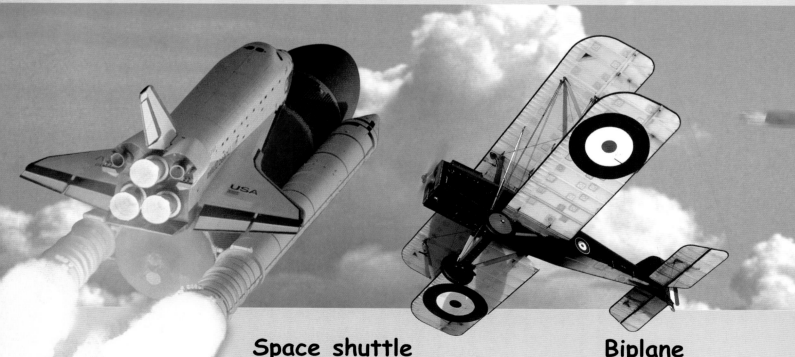

Space shuttle

There are four space shuttles. Each was designed to fly 100 missions.

Biplane

A biplane's open cockpit means the pilot needs a warm hat, scarf, gloves, jacket—and goggles.

Pitts stunt plane

These biplanes were the most popular aerobatic planes in the 1950s and 1960s.

Ultralight

An ultralight's propeller turns around about 1,500 times a minute.

Air-to-air refueling

A second form of air-to-air refueling uses a rigid boom instead of a drogue basket.

Emmly Masanabo

Chinook

There are about 300 control buttons and switches on the flight deck of this Chinook.

Jumbo jet

You could park 45 family-sized cars on the wings of a jumbo jet.

Glossary

Amphibian is an airplane that can operate on land and water.

Control tower is a tall airport building. The people inside direct the aircraft flying into and out of the airport.

Flight deck is the cockpit of the airplane where the pilot and copilot operate the flight controls.

Fuselage is the main body of an airplane that holds the crew, passengers, and luggage.

Orbiter is the spacecraft part of a space shuttle; the part that holds the astronauts.

Payload bay is the part of the orbiter that holds the satellite or other equipment needed for a mission.

Propeller is the rotating blade on some aircraft. The propellers are driven by the engine and power the plane through the air.

Runway is a strip of ground where airplanes can take off or land.

Thermals are rising bodies of warm air. A glider uses thermals to stay up.

Throttle is a mechanism on the flight deck that controls the flow of fuel to the plane's engines, which allows the pilot to control his speed.

Vapor trail is the visible stream released behind an airplane. The stream is water vapor.

Yoke is the control device on the flight deck that the pilot and copilot use to steer the plane.

Index

Airliner coming in to land

Acknowledgments

Dorling Kindersley would like to thank:
Fleur Star for preparing the index and assisting with the glossary; and Rebecca Sodergren for picture library services.

Picture credits:

The publisher would like to thank the following for their kind permission to reproduce their photographs:

a=above; c=center; b=below; l=left; r=right; t=top;
1: Richard Cooke; 2-3: Richard Cooke; 4: Corbis/Kevin Fleming tl; Robert Harding Picture Library crb; 4-5: Austin Brown/Aviation Picture Library; 6: Corbis/Kevin Fleming tl; 6-7: Corbis/ George Hall; 7: Aviation Images tl; 7: Getty photodisc/Jack Hollingsworth cra; 8-9: The Flight Collection; 10: Corbis/Adrian Carroll/Eye Ubiquitous tl; 10-11: Corbis/Eric Curry; 11: Austin Brown/Aviation Picture Library tr; 12: Austin Brown/Aviation Picture Library br; ; 12-13: Austin Brown/Aviation Picture Library; 13: Airsport Photo Library/Guy Westgate tr; 14: Aviation Images/John Dibbs cl; Aviation Images/Mark Wagner br; 14-15: Corbis/Chris Simpson/Cordaiy Photo Library Ltd; 16: Aviation Images/Mark Wagner bl; 16-17: Getty Images/Jean AEF.Duboisberranger; 18-19: Corbis/James A. Sugar; 19: Corbis/Bettmann cr; Robert Harding Picture Library/Ian Griffiths tc; 20: Corbis/Bob Krist cl; Corbis/Tim Wright cl; 20-21: Corbis/Paul A. Souders;. 21: Corbis/Tim Wright r; 22: Aviation Images tr; Corbis cr; 23: Aviation Images; 24: Robert Harding Picture Library tr; 24-25: Aviation Images/Mark Wagner; 26: NASA cl; 26-27: NASA c, b; 27: NASA cr, br; 28: Corbis cl; 28-29: Aviation Images/John Dibbs c; Richard Cooke t; 29: Aviation Images/Mark Wagner cra; 30: Aviation Images tl; Aviation Images/John Dibbs br; Corbis/Carol Havers tc; Corbis/Joseph Sohm/ChromoSohm Inc tr; NASA bl; 31: Austin Brown/Aviation Picture Library tc, br; Corbis/George Hall tr; 32: Corbis/David Lawrence bl; eps: alamy.com/ Steve Bloom Images; Jacket: front main picture: FTOP Pte. Ltd., Singapore Colin Koh; back cover background shot: FTOP Pte. Ltd., Singapore

All other images © Dorling Kindersley
For further information see: www.dkimages.com